Moon Magic

Journal

Harness the Power of the Lunar Cycles with
Guided Rituals, Spells & Meditations

AURORA KANE

WELLFLEET
PRESS

The Moon's soft light invites you here, to sit and gaze in awe
at what her magic offers you in matters great and small.

Her guiding grace and wisdom true are wise beyond her years;
her charming sight, a sure delight, can calm your greatest fears.

Her beacon lights the path we chart; her shadows mark the spot
to stop and listen carefully to what is in our heart—

For there lies magic deep and true—it burns with brightest light
revealing hopes and dreams and strengths unseen until this night.

Where peace, and joy, and honesty align intentions' might
rejoice in what you find within, no others are alike.

*Blessed be those who enter these pages with open mind
and open heart. The magic is yours for the taking.*

CONTENTS

Journaling with the Moon ☾ 5

Astrology and the Moon ☾ 15

Phase 1: New Moon ☾ 25

Phase 2: Waxing Crescent ☾ 39

Phase 3: First Quarter Moon ☾ 53

Phase 4: Waxing Gibbous ☾ 67

Phase 5: Full Moon ☾ 81

Phase 6: Waning Gibbous ☾ 111

Phase 7: Last (Third) Quarter Moon ☾ 125

Phase 8: Waning Crescent, or Balsamic Moon ☾ 139

Your Moon Magic Journey ☾ 152

Use this space to freely record your affirmations.

MEDITATING WITH THE MOON

Journaling and meditation can be significant ways to reach our inner thoughts and feelings and identify where our intentions lie. Meditating with the Moon helps elevate our human existence into a sacred realm and clear the clutter that can accumulate in our brains. Use this present moment to focus on your breathing. When ready, close your eyes and open your arms to Mother Moon—and allow her to take you into hers.

What led you to this journey with the Moon?

THE POWER OF COLOR

Color has its own energy and can be used to enhance the Moon's powerful vibrations. Weave the magic of color into your Moon spells and rituals.

BLACK
to protect from negative energy

GREEN
for growth, money, good luck, abundance, success

RED and PINK
for love, passion, friendship, forgiveness

YELLOW,
for personal power and self-esteem, realizing and manifesting intentions, confidence, mental clarity, intuition

ORANGE and GOLD
for energy, creativity, attraction

WHITE, SILVER, and GRAY
for truth and clairvoyance

BLUE
for tranquility, patience, kindness, meditation, sincerity

LAVENDER
for protection, intuition, peace, spiritual growth

How will you use your favorite color to enhance your Moon magic intentions?

THE POWERFUL MAGIC OF THE MOON

The magnificent, magical, mystical Moon is often referred to as the Triple Goddess, characterized as a female passing through life's phases—from young woman, to adult woman and mother, and, finally, to the old woman, or crone. It takes about twenty-nine days for the Moon to pass through all eight phases. Each phase of the Moon presents an opportunity to invite its purposeful energy into our life and reflect it back to the Universe in manifesting our goals.

Phases 1 through 5, from New Moon to Full Moon—the Moon's *waxing* phases, when she grows to full power—are the ideal phases to work your magic to draw things to you. Phases 5 through 1, from Full Moon back to New Moon—the Moon's *waning* phases, when her light diminishes and the monthly cycle ends—are times for reflection, assessment, and removing and releasing harmful energies from your Universe. Note, to those in the Southern Hemisphere, the phases appear reversed.

In my life, I want to draw more

_____

_____

_____

_____

I want to release

_____

_____

_____

_____

What excites you most about the possibilities you can uncover in the Moon's magical light? How will you use the Moon's magic in your daily life?

Astrology and the Moon

Journaling with the Moon's energetic phases and astrology as superpowers can enhance our vibrations, awareness, and intuition. Each Zodiac sign comprises traits that influence your personality and carries a corresponding element—fire, air, water, or earth.

> ☽ If your sign is a **fire** or an **air** sign, you tend toward positive/extroverted (masculine) tendencies.

> ☽ **Water** and **earth** signs are the opposite—feminine, grounded, and intuitive.

As the Full Moon recurs throughout the year, traveling through each sign of the Zodiac, the personality traits associated with that sign are amplified—and felt by those whose intuition is attuned enough to notice, not just those with that birth sign. The following list offers a snapshot of each sign's significant traits—the good and not so good. Find yours and consider, during the next Full Moon, which traits will be on full display, as well as those that may need, well, a little extra management to stay in the moment and live your best, most purposeful life. Set your intentions accordingly and open yourself to the power of the Full Moon.

ARIES, *The Ram*

(March 21–April 20); fire sign

Let the Full Moon's Glow Show:
confidence, courage, determination

See the Truth in the Full Moon's Light:
aggressiveness, impatience, moodiness

GEMINI, *The Twins*

(May 22–June 21); air sign

Let the Full Moon's Glow Show: charm,
curiosity, friendliness, gentleness

See the Truth in the Full Moon's Light:
inconsistency, indecision, nervousness

TAURUS, *The Bull*

(April 21–May 21); earth sign

Let the Full Moon's Glow Show:
patience, practicality, reliability

See the Truth in the Full Moon's
Light: possessiveness, stubbornness,
uncompromising

CANCER, *The Crab*

(June 22–July 22); water sign

Let the Full Moon's Glow Show: bravery,
loyalty, nurturing

See the Truth in the Full Moon's Light:
moodiness, defensiveness, insecurity

LEO, *The Lion*

(July 23–August 22); fire sign

Let the Full Moon's Glow Show: pride, creativity, warmheartedness

See the Truth in the Full Moon's Light: arrogance, inflexibility, stubbornness

LIBRA, *The Scales*

(September 24–October 23); air sign

Let the Full Moon's Glow Show: cooperation, fair-mindedness, graciousness

See the Truth in the Full Moon's Light: frivolity, indecision, controlling

VIRGO, *The Maiden*

(August 23–September 23); earth sign

Let the Full Moon's Glow Show: analytical, insightful, productive

See the Truth in the Full Moon's Light: anxious, critical, no fun

SCORPIO, *The Scorpion*

(October 24–November 22); water sign

Let the Full Moon's Glow Show: bravery, passion, resiliency

See the Truth in the Full Moon's Light: emotional, jealously, secrecy

SAGITTARIUS,
The Centaur

(November 23–December 21); fire sign

Let the Full Moon's Glow Show:
adventurousness, generosity, intelligence

See the Truth in the Full Moon's Light:
impatience, overpromises, rudeness

AQUARIUS,
The Water Bearer

(January 21–February 19)

Let the Full Moon's Glow Show:
generosity, humanity, perceptiveness,
tolerance

See the Truth in the Full Moon's
Light: aloof, inability to compromise,
temperamental

CAPRICORN,
The Mountain Goat

(December 22–January 20); earth sign

Let the Full Moon's Glow Show:
analytical, discipline, leadership

See the Truth in the Full Moon's Light:
condescending, know-it-all, selfish

PISCES,
The Fish

(February 20–March 20), water sign

Let the Full Moon's Glow Show: artistic,
compassion, dreamer, intuitive

See the Truth in the Full Moon's Light:
indecision, overly trusting, worry

Based on your Zodiac sign, what personal traits do you feel are influenced by the Full Moon? How do you use this energy to bring more magic into your life?

_____

_____

_____

_____

_____

_____

_____

_____

_____

_____

Lunar Personality Type

The specific _lunar phase_ you were born under can reveal magic influences at work in your life—especially during that specific Moon phase. It's easy to find the Moon phase you were born under by searching online for "moon phase" + your birthday (month/day/year) + country born in. Consider your birth Moon phase to understand your ideas, emotions, behaviors, and traits more deeply, then those of friends and family for insight into what may influence your relationships.

New Moon: Though the sky is dark, if you were born under this Moon phase, your personality is bright and enthusiastic. You are excited about new beginnings and open to the potential ahead. Your excitement translates to creativity, hard work, and success, but practice self-care to avoid burnout.

What self-care practices keep you balanced and protected from going at things too hard? How can you incorporate the energies of the New Moon into your practice?

Waxing Moon Phases: *Waxing Crescent, First Quarter, Waxing Gibbous:* The waxing phases are all about growth. Those born under these phases are positive, trusting, confident, goal-oriented, and comfortable in the world. *Waxing Crescent* babies are particularly creative; those born under *the First Quarter Moon* tend to be very strong-willed, and the *Waxing Gibbous* baby shines the light of compassion for others.

What is your strategy for dealing with the roadblocks life can present that can derail your progress toward achieving your goals?

Full Moon: Born under the Full Moon means you're all about manifestation and achieving goals. While your passion drives you forward, you have the unique gift of being able to look back and turn the lessons learned into new accomplishments. Although you are quick to master skills and proceed to the next challenge, take time to sit with your thoughts and feelings to be sure your decisions are solid.

Describe how you feel when the Moon is full. How does that compare with what you observe in friends and family?

Waning Moon Phases: *Gibbous, Last (Third) Quarter, Waning Crescent:*
If born under one of the waning phases, you are comfortable with yourself
and a calming, healing influence on others. You forgive easily. Those born
under a *Waning Gibbous Moon* are naturally reflective and adept at teaching
others from their own experiences. Born under the *Last (Third) Quarter
Moon,* you are wise beyond your years and eager to help others by sharing
your wisdom. If the *Waning Crescent* accompanied you into this world, your
journey will be one of endings and new beginnings, coupled with an intuitive
ability to navigate them successfully.

The waning phases are about release and closure. How can you use your
natural wisdom to help others know when it's time to let go of things that no
longer serve their greater good?

What self-care ritual can you adopt, or continue purposefully, to maintain the fresh, invigorating spirit the New Moon brings?

As you set intentions with the New Moon, how can you honor Earth for keeping you grounded and supported in your journey?

What is it about your intentions that excites you to work toward your goals?

What do you want to accomplish?

How will you know when your intentions have manifested?

PHASE 2
Waxing Crescent

With less than one-quarter of the Moon visible, this is a renewing period of continually growing light, which illuminates intentions and intuition. This is a time of gathering energy, with a summons to action to actually *do* something to complete those things you've put aside because they're hard or uncomfortable. The Moon's growing light corresponds to your growing determination to meet goals and challenges. Commit to what you can achieve, but do so knowing fully *why* your goal is important. This phase is also said to be a good time to plant crops—"in the light of the Moon"—the original seeds of intention!

MOON MAGIC TOOLBOX

Wear lavender or yellow for confidence and invite the Moon's protective embrace. Burn a white candle while journaling to boost your goddess wisdom and intuition and give you the courage to listen to your heart.

Reflect on your courage to face the unknown and write an affirmation celebrating your undaunted self in pursuing your goals.

_____

_____

_____

_____

WAXING CRESCENT SPELL

Evoke the gathering energies of the Waxing Crescent Moon as you journal about your growing intentions. Say quietly or aloud:

When Goddess Moon begins to smile, she lights the evening sky,
Where nestled in those growing beams I journal my desires.
For with your help, that spark of joy will fast ignite my fire
that dreams come, as told to you, with hard work you've inspired.

What is holding you back from committing to your dreams?

_____

_____

_____

_____

_____

_____

_____

_____

_____

_____

_____

WAXING CRESCENT MEDITATION

Use this meditation to help you align your energies and better attract what you want. If you want to add essential oils to your meditation, try lemon or common sage essential oil. The aromas will cleanse and clear your mind and spirit. Find a comfortable place to sit and take some deep, cleansing, relaxing breaths—in, then out. Continue until you feel grounded and ready to begin. Imagine your favorite place: a forest, a beach, someplace relaxing and full of possibilities, wonder, and total acceptance. Allow your breathing to find a rhythm. Think of the expansive sky with its glittering stars, depth of mystery, and universal magic. How can you bring this magic into your life?

What actions will you take today to step toward your intentions?

HEALING ENERGY RITUAL:
THE LAW OF VIBRATION

The law of vibration is the foundation of the law of attraction and tells us every "thing" vibrates—and everything in the Universe, being made differently, vibrates at different frequencies. Some frequencies are obvious (think: color or music), but some are not. What is obvious, though, is that these energies are interconnected and influenced by each other, as ripples in a pond. And those ripples can send positive energy and vibrations anywhere in the world they're needed—and, multiplied by like energy, return to you in abundance.

- ❯ When something happens that particularly touches you, find time to sit quietly and journal about your thoughts.

- ❯ Gather matches and candles in any color reflecting your message or intentions (see page 11).

- ❯ Place the candle on a heatproof surface. Visualize your good and healing intentions being transferred into the candle. Light the candle.

- ❯ With a soft focus on the candle's flame as it releases the energy of your message, visualize your intentions being manifested. Pray for pain to be eased or light to be given.

- ❯ Let the candle burn. Extinguish it. Give thanks to the Universe for your place in it.

What healing message would you like to extend to the Universe? How do you envision the outcome?

MOON MAGIC REFLECTIONS

Does your intention feel true? What steps are needed to manifest your intentions?

What actions have you taken towards your intentions? Which have been successful, and which haven't?

What does the Waxing Crescent Moon inspire in you?

What colors are you drawn to during this Moon cycle? What can they help you achieve?

What change in your life do you seek to manifest? How will you get there?

What positive habits have you been or will you begin practicing to invite more positive change into your life?

As the Moon grows larger during this cycle, how can you think "larger" about your intentions?

What have you learned? What has surprised you? Write freely about anything on your mind.

PHASE 3
First Quarter Moon

Though a Quarter Moon in name, this glowing beacon in the sky shows fully half its surface lit and has progressed halfway to a Full Moon. The "quarter" in her name tells us the Moon is one-fourth of the way through her cycle around the Earth. This Moon phase is a time of emotional balance and confidence. It's a time to nurture relationships and tend to that love, which also may require pruning a few branches. It also signals a time of full-on action. As the energies of change are at work, they can sometimes drag us along without our consent, so remain committed but flexible and be ready to make decisions, as needed.

MOON MAGIC TOOLBOX

The Magician tarot card is the card of the First Quarter Moon. It bridges the spiritual and worldly realms and creates using willpower and aspiration. Use the card's message to spur you toward your goals.

Write an affirmation honoring your self-confidence to take action to achieve your goals and keep it front of mind.

_____

_____

_____

FIRST QUARTER MOON SPELL

Evoke the energies of the First Quarter Moon as you journal about your plan for manifesting intentions. Say quietly or aloud:

Universal truth.

Actions convey our essence.

Moonbeams never cease.

What specific steps toward reaching your goals will you take next?

_____

_____

_____

_____

_____

_____

_____

_____

_____

_____

FIRST QUARTER MOON MEDITATION

Before you get ready to take action on your intentions, find a comfortable spot to sit or lie down. To enhance your meditation, light a yellow candle before beginning. Yellow is great for mental clarity and boosting personal power. Take one deep breath in through your nose and exhale through your mouth. Continue breathing evenly while gently turning your focus to the rhythm of your breath. Take a moment to meditate on your intentions and experience any feelings they bring up. Use this time to work through any obstacles that may be in your path.

Where have you made progress?

CREATE A SACRED SPACE RITUAL

This First Quarter Moon phase is one of balance and confidence . . . so, claim your sacred space as your own. Your sacred space can include an altar or just offer a peaceful space for you to be. If you already have a sacred space, tidy and cleanse it and evaluate, remove, and replace any objects currently in it to reset and recharge the energy of your space. If not, it's easy to create one:

❭ Select a private space where you can journal and meditate undisturbed—it does not need to be a separate room; even a chair or table in a quiet corner works.

❭ Thoroughly tidy and cleanse the space to clear any negative energy. Burn common sage, spritz a smudge spray, or use a sage branch to sprinkle Moon water (see page 84) around the space for a ceremonial energy cleanse, if you wish. Open any nearby windows to release the negativity.

❭ If establishing an altar, set out any objects that are important to you and place each object with gratitude and intention.

❭ Create atmosphere with music and lighting, if you like.

❭ Add a comfortable chair or pillows and a place to write.

❭ Create an affirmation that calls you to the space and affirms its purpose in your life. Each time, before using your sacred space, start with a few cleansing, centering breaths. Evoke your affirmation, quietly or aloud. Close your session with a moment of gratitude for the Moon's guidance and the abundance in your life.

As the Moon's phases change over time, so, too, will your use of this space . . . write your sacred space affirmation . . . one that affirms its purpose in your life and celebrates your intentions. Revise as needed!

MOON MAGIC REFLECTIONS

What new projects have you been dreaming of launching? Now's the time.
What will you do to make them a reality?

What insecurities may be keeping you from moving forward and how can you face them?

Reflect carefully on decisions to be made during this time. What decisions are you struggling with? What will help you determine the path forward?

As this Moon phase is an active one, what physical activity can you engage in to keep up the energy?

What is the most courageous thing you've done recently and how did it make you feel?

How have you changed along this Moon magic journey?

What have you learned from the missteps along the way?

Make a list of all the opportunities you'd like to accept, then prioritize them based on your intentions.

Waxing Gibbous

As the Waxing Gibbous Moon grows in illumination, so does the energy to manifest hopes and dreams. This is the phase devoted to attracting to you what you desire and refining your efforts to achieve it. Whatever your intentions—friends, money, health, protection, travel, business success— clear the path and continue your progress. Though the light is brighter, you may have trouble seeing how your desired results will materialize. Continue the hard work that fuels your passion. Trust your instincts and know that you, alone, have what it takes to realize your dreams.

MOON MAGIC TOOLBOX

Tiger's eye can increase your ability to see, observe, and sense. This gemstone's energies align naturally with the Moon's Waxing Gibbous phase, when energy and excitement build, and a little clarity can offer another perspective.

Create an affirmation that turns your fear into power to recognize opportunity and draw it to you.

WAXING GIBBOUS SPELL

Evoke the energies of the Waxing Gibbous while holding a tiger's eye, if you have one, for a clear perspective, then say quietly or aloud:

I stand beneath your growing light and ask for growing courage
To boldly see what lies ahead and move toward it undeterred.
For much as change can bring delight, it sometimes can be feared.
With heart of faith, I pray your gaze doth light this path I've cleared.

What's left to do to manifest your intentions? Invite the Moon to walk the final steps with you.

WAXING GIBBOUS MEDITATION

Use this meditation to focus your intentions and nurture your wishes. Before beginning, consider making yourself a soothing herbal tea using basil, ginseng, rosemary, or thyme to help calm your mind before meditating. Pick a comfortable spot and sit or lie down there. Slowly close your eyes as you breathe in deeply. Hold your breath for a count of 2, then exhale for a count of 2, releasing any worry, fear, or doubt with your exhale. As you do, visualize your dreams manifesting in your life. What do they look like? What does it feel like? Stay there for a moment. Then say to yourself, "I believe and trust myself to manifest anything I put my mind to." Take one final deep breath in, hold for a count of 2, and release your breath for a count of 2.

Is there something still holding you back? How can you move past it?

MOON CIRCLE RITUAL:
ATTRACTING POSITIVE ENERGIES

Your circle is your sacred space to work your magic. Create it with physical objects, such as crystals or stones, or simply draw it in the air with your finger. It is a powerful place to gather and create energy.

❭ Gather your friends under the next Waxing Gibbous Moon to connect and amplify their manifesting energies by joining hands in the circle, standing or sitting around an altar, if you wish.

❭ If desired, each person can place an object to be charged with the Moon's energy inside the circle or on the altar. The purpose of your circle is to celebrate and honor the Goddess Moon and all her gifts, to open yourself to her light, increasing energy, and intuition.

❭ Use the circle to draw the Waxing Gibbous Moon's abundant energies to you. Create and chant your own mantra to raise the energies around you.

❭ Stand or sit silently in meditation on your intentions, which are about to manifest.

❭ Sing, or dance clockwise in the circle.

❭ Light a candle in memory of someone who isn't there.

❭ When it's time to bring the circle to a close, take a moment to give thanks for the many blessings bestowed by the Moon and the blessing of friends.

❭ Walk or dance counterclockwise to dissolve the circle.

❭ Continue on your path. Do not let doubts derail your progress. Blessed be.

The Moon is your constant companion and friend, offering her wisdom and guidance. How can you bring more positivity into your life to reach your goals?

MOON MAGIC REFLECTIONS

Describe the feelings you have about the work you've been doing to manifest your intentions.

What has been the most difficult part? Why do you think that is?

What has been the most rewarding part? Why do you think that is?

You've almost realized your goal. How will you feel when you've achieved the intentions you set with the New Moon?

Describe the most magical insight the Moon's illuminating power has shown you. How do you use the information?

How have you grown, along with the Moon, in your magical journey?

Describe a time you procrastinated on finishing something because you were afraid of what was next.

How are you living your most magical life?

Full Moon

The Full Moon is a time in the Moon's cycle full of energy and abundance. It is a time for celebrating achievements realized and giving gratitude for blessings; it is also a time of cleansing and letting go, of releasing what no longer serves our purpose. The Full Moon was historically a significant source of light at night, guiding travelers across uncharted seas or unfamiliar meadows, and allowing work to continue later in the day as the harvest grew near. Harness that unique power to bring clarity to your life and positive energy to all you do. There is great opportunity awaiting.

MOON MAGIC TOOLBOX

Wearing, or carrying, your birthstone is said to bring luck and good health—and an extra dose of magic. And, if your birthday falls anywhere near or on the Full Moon, prepare for a year of big accomplishments. You can easily find your birthstone by searching online for your birthday or birth month + birthstone.

Write a Full Moon affirmation that celebrates your achievement and hard work during this Moon's phase.

_____

_____

_____

FULL MOON SPELL

Evoke the Full Moon's glorious energies as you journal about manifesting intentions. Say quietly or aloud:

> *When Full Moon rises in the sky, so rise the tides on Earth.*
> *To feel the music shift and swell results in joyous mirth.*
> *To ride the waves I manifest I must not fear or doubt,*
> *But trim my sails to catch the wind, to guide my ship full out.*

How will you celebrate achieving your goals?

_____

_____

_____

_____

_____

_____

_____

_____

_____

_____

FULL MOON MEDITATION

Find a comfortable spot to sit and begin to gently center yourself: focus on your breath and relax into your chair. If you have a citrine or moldavite crystal, hold it or keep it near as you meditate. A citrine can bring energies of optimism and prosperity, perfect for a time of abundance. Moldavite is said to bring healing and increases intuition. When you feel grounded, begin to visualize yourself walking through an outdoor space, such as a park, under the Moon's full light, filling yourself with fresh air and the joy that Nature brings. Feel the ground beneath your feet and the breeze against your cheek. Imagine yourself stretching, making yourself as big as you can, just like the Moon. Raise your arms to the Moon in thanks for her powers and guidance. Do a dance in celebration.

What positive things has the Full Moon illuminated in your life?

MOON WATER RITUAL

Take advantage of the Full Moon's heightened energy to conjure a cauldron full of Moon water. Its uses are many in your magical life:

- ❱ Add the water to a Moon bath ritual.

- ❱ Immerse your water-safe crystals in it to cleanse and reenergize them.

- ❱ Cleanse the aura of a room using an herb sprig, branch, or bundle to scatter the water charged with the Full Moon's energy around your home for protection and blessing.

- ❱ Put some fresh basil or rosemary leaves in it, along with some lemon slices, and cleanse the floors of your home for health and good luck.

- ❱ Use it to make a smudging spray.

While the wise Moon displays her most vibrant power, fill a large, lidded container with water and place it outside where it can catch the Moon's beams, or indoors near a window that receives the Moon's light. Cover the container. Take a moment to focus your intentions into the water, then let it bathe in the Moon's nourishing energy. The next day, the water is ready to use. Label it and keep refrigerated, if you wish.

What achievements are you celebrating and what is their significance in your life?

Living a magical life in tune with Nature means offering gratitude for her gifts. What are you grateful for and why?

What, in the light of the Full Moon, seems least useful to you now that might surprise you? Why do you think this is?

Have you ever behaved in unexplainable ways during the influence of the Full Moon? Describe what happened.

How will you use the Full Moon's power to achieve your desires?

SIGNIFICANCE OF THE SEASONAL FULL MOONS

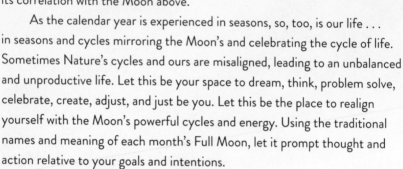

In North America, as the Moon led us through the yearly cycle, Native Americans, who also used the Moon as a calendar to track the seasons, assigned symbolic names to each month's Full Moon based on their observations of Nature and its correlation with the Moon above.

As the calendar year is experienced in seasons, so, too, is our life . . . in seasons and cycles mirroring the Moon's and celebrating the cycle of life. Sometimes Nature's cycles and ours are misaligned, leading to an unbalanced and unproductive life. Let this be your space to dream, think, problem solve, celebrate, create, adjust, and just be you. Let this be the place to realign yourself with the Moon's powerful cycles and energy. Using the traditional names and meaning of each month's Full Moon, let it prompt thought and action relative to your goals and intentions.

What do you love most about yourself?

JANUARY: Wolf Moon / Old Moon

January's cold and dark leave Nature's food sources in scarce supply. Howling, hungry wolves emerging from hibernation are said to be the inspiration for the name of January's Moon. Winter's Moons, from January through March, watch over a time of returning inside and turning inward in reflection. It is a time of rest and renewal.

Meditate in the quiet stillness of January's Moon and record your thoughts and observations here. Did you feel anything unexpected?

FEBRUARY: Snow Moon / Hunger Moon

A typical time of heavy snowfall in many parts of North America gave this midwinter Moon her fitting name. The snow, in turn, made hunting difficult, meaning food was scare, resulting in the hunger-related moniker. Though winter continues in full force, daylight hours are gently increasing as we move toward spring. With colder temperatures in many areas, and increased time inside, bask in the Full Moon's glow while observing Nature's beautiful winter landscape.

How will you show appreciation for your individual beauty and gifts at this time?

LUNAR ECLIPSES

Lunar eclipses happen during a Full Moon, when the Sun, Earth, and Moon align. Earth blocks the Sun's light from reaching the Moon and so it appears dark when passing through Earth's shadow. Eclipses are Nature's way of getting our attention—they shake us out of "the routine" and spark transformation. These are times of demarcation, usually signifying an ending and significant, often unexpected, change. Emotions can run high during an eclipse, and so it may not be the best time for decisive action. Open your mind to your intuition while journaling. Listen to messages received from all parts of your life.

What do you need to forgive or let go of to move peacefully into the changes initiated by the lunar eclipse?

_____

_____

_____

_____

_____

_____

_____

Waning Gibbous

As the Waning Gibbous Moon passes into this dimming phase, it signals a slowing down of sorts, affording us time for reflection and assessment of lessons learned. Review what went well and what went wrong and share your story for the benefit of others. Express gratitude for the chance to learn and grow. It is a time for abandoning old habits, easing the stress of working toward your goals, and amping up affirmations to counter negative self-talk for what was not achieved. This is also the time to dissolve unproductive relationships or recharge existing ones. It is a time to clear the mind of clutter. It is also a beginning phase of renewal, so we can embrace the opportunities that lie ahead.

MOON MAGIC TOOLBOX

Rose quartz is the crystal of unconditional love and compassion and is best used during the Waning Gibbous phase, fostering feelings of love, gratitude, and peace as we see our intentions manifest.

Inspired by the Moon's love for all who seek her wisdom, write an affirmation celebrating all there is to love about you.

_____

_____

_____

WANING GIBBOUS SPELL

Evoke the grateful energies of the Waning Gibbous Moon as you prepare to journal under her calming influence. Say quietly or aloud:

Dear Moon above, with love below, I'm grateful for what life bestows.
With moonbeams gathered in my arms, I feel the blessings of your charms.
And lessons learned while in your grace, ensure the world's a better place.

How can you use the lessons of the Waning Gibbous Moon to make the world a better place?

_____

_____

_____

_____

_____

_____

_____

_____

_____

_____

WANING GIBBOUS MEDITATION

To find more clarity during this phase, find a quiet, comfortable place. If you can, wear or safely diffuse clary sage, lavender, or rose essential oil during your meditation practice. These relaxing oils can help you feel more open to receiving the Moon's messages. Take a deep breath, feel your belly expand with the breath, then slowly exhale. As you continue to breathe, reflect on your journey so far. Recall where you began the journey and recognize the progress you've made. This is a time to be thankful for what the Moon has inspired in you. Take one last deep breath in and exhale it into stillness. Take a moment to thank yourself for continuing your path.

What part of your journey are you most thankful for?

MOON TEA: A SOOTHING RITUAL

Follow the centuries-old traditions of herbal medicine working to heal what ails and concoct a batch of Moon tea to drink daily to refresh your intentions, or incorporate into your Moon rituals and intention setting. Making the tea blends yourself, rather than using purchased tea bags (which, of course, are fine if that's what you have and prefer), offers a way to slow down and focus on the process. Give thanks to the plants that provide the ingredients.

) Use 2 to 3 teaspoons of a dried herb or herb blend per cup (8 ounces, or 240 ml) of tea. For larger quantities, say a 1 gallon (3.8 L), use about 1 cup (weight varies) of dried herbs.

) If you use fresh herbs, *grown without pesticides*, those gathered under the Moon's light will be even more inspiring—place a big handful (a single herb or a mix) into a large pot or clean coffeepot. Use mint for cleansing and healing. Jasmine reduces fear and eases transitions. Marjoram brews confidence and courage.

) When ready to brew your cuppa, boil as much Moon water (see page 84) as needed and steep your tea (in a strainer, tea ball, clean unscented muslin bag, or disposable filter) for about 5 minutes.

) Close your eyes, inhale the soothing aromas, and take time to meditate on its soothing scent.

) Taste and adjust the herb quantity and steep time as needed. Sweeten with dried fruits, spices, honey, or dried culinary flowers, like rose petals, as desired.

Describe a ritual, like teatime, that is a family tradition you cherish. Is there room for new rituals in your life? What would they be?

MOON MAGIC REFLECTIONS

What lessons learned have been most valuable while working through this Moon phase?

How can you use those lessons to guide others?

What has the Waning Gibbous Moon revealed to you about compassion?

Why might the Waning Gibbous phase be a favorite phase for you?

Describe a time someone showed great compassion for you. How did it make you feel? How have you honored that act of kindness?

How do you define "Moon magic"?

As this Moon cycle comes to a close, what do you still feel needs closure in your life?

What bad habits have you kicked to the curb to make room for more joy in your life?

Last (Third) Quarter Moon

This Last (Third) Quarter Moon is a time of release and regrouping. This phase is one of responsibility. Recognize your missteps and shift your thinking to align with your intentions. Now is a time to attend to unfinished business, make amends, and spend some energy on self-care. Reflect on past experiences, while considering future action. This is a time of cleansing—physically and emotionally—to freely let go of anything that is not a positive force in your life or that obstructs your goals, including your own disappointment. Stop negative thoughts, let go of hurtful habits, and remove obstacles or negative people from your path. The Last (Third) Quarter Moon is an especially good time to invite forgiveness in.

MOON MAGIC TOOLBOX

A cast-iron cauldron symbolizes rebirth and feminine energy. If you have a cauldron on your altar, carefully burn wishes and intentions to set them free to manifest.

Write an affirmation of self-forgiveness that acknowledges what needs forgiving and offers unconditional love.

LAST (THIRD) QUARTER SPELL

Evoke the reflective energies of the Last (Third) Quarter Moon as you continue to journal. Say quietly or aloud:

What better time to chat, dear Moon, your friendship has its perks.
For striving so has left me, though, a bit stressed and in search . . .
Of ways to gather courage to say, "We tried our best, but failed."
For lessons learned can pave the way to even greater works.

What are some boundaries you have set up for yourself to ensure you take time for self-care?

LAST (THIRD) QUARTER
MOON MEDITATION

As you work on releasing anything that is not serving you, use this meditation to help you move forward in peace. On a steady surface, light a candle— rose or pink for harmony and forgiveness, or black for protection against negative energies. Find a comfortable place to sit and begin to focus on your breathing. Slowly shift your focus to your body as you do a quick scan from head to toe. Do you feel tension? Pain? Fatigue? Identify what you need to release. Now, imagine breathing in a soothing light, directing it toward the places in your body that need ease. Focus your breath on a specific spot until the tension, pain, or unease releases. Continue until you are fully relaxed and at ease. Use this time to forgive yourself and others.

How will your Moon magic journey be improved because of what you're letting go?

SUNSET CEREMONY RITUAL

Anger, fear, shame, and resentment are not your friends in Moon magic—or life. They block your magical energy flow and can literally make you sick. It's time for some self-care in the form of forgiveness. All that's needed is a red rose and a place to view the sunset.

> Outside, if you can, stand in view of the developing sunset. Take a moment to ground yourself and focus on your intention to forgive. Visualize the person you forgive. This may feel hard. That's okay.

> As the sky glows glorious red, pink, blue, orange, lavender, peach, and more, fully inhale the healing energies of the calming colors. Let them absorb any hurt and anger. Exhale your hurt, fear, and resentment. Inhale the colors again, individually, and let them fill you with joy. Exhale forgiveness into the world.

> If tears appear during this step, let them flow. They are healing and a release. One by one, remove the petals from the rose. Toss them to the wind and say:

I forgive [name]. I no longer ache. I no longer cry. I am love. I am free to forgive.

> When all the petals have been dispersed, stand in the breeze and feel it wash over you, taking away any remaining hurt with the petals.

> Take a moment to recognize the hard work you've done and be grateful for the new beginning you just gave yourself. Bow to the Sun in thanks; raise your hands in prayer to the Moon. Blessed be.

How does true forgiveness make you feel?

MOON MAGIC REFLECTIONS

Journal about a time you needed to be forgiven. Did you forgive yourself?
(Hint: It might be time to, if you haven't.)

What did you learn about yourself through this journey?

What should you give up or release for your greater good, but that you might be afraid to?

What unfinished business should you attend to at this time?

Describe your recent dreams. Look for patterns. What do you think they're trying to tell you?

What things are you naturally drawn to these days that seem out of the ordinary? Is there a message there?

Mastering your life is achieved by mastering the lessons it teaches and using them to grow. What lessons have resonated with your most during this Moon phase?

Do your commitments align with your priorities and bring you joy and satisfaction?

PHASE 8
Waning Crescent, or Balsamic Moon

Also called the Old Moon or Balsamic Moon, this end of the lunar cycle is a time of renewal, inward reflection, and self-awareness, in thoughtful darkness, as a new cycle begins. When the last sliver of the Waning Crescent Moon hangs in the night sky, it signals a time of rest, of thanks for gifts received, of recognizing what no longer serves our higher good. It is a time for spellwork and journaling with a focus on release and letting go, banishment, and breaking bad habits, including bad relationships. Embrace the significance of this bittersweet life phase—often a solitary one—and accept the wisdom of your experience as the guiding force it is.

MOON MAGIC TOOLBOX

During the Waning Crescent, evoke any of the crone goddesses to help deal with letting go, or life's transformations. Powerful crystal allies in this are amethyst, for its guiding properties, and clear quartz, which ignites change.

Write an affirmation about letting the negative, unhelpful parts of your life go, with gratitude for when they did serve, or honoring your inner goddess.

WANING CRESCENT MOON SPELL

Evoke the intuitive energies of the Waning Crescent Moon as you begin to journal. Say quietly or aloud:

> *Quiet darkness offers rest. I take the chance to breathe.*
> *To thank myself for showing up and giving life my best.*
> *I gather near all I hold dear, which fuels me for the rest.*

What no longer serves your purpose or adds positivity to your life?

WANING CRESCENT, OR
BALSAMIC MOON, MEDITATION

As you look within, use this meditation to reflect on your journey. Before starting, make yourself a cup of tea with chamomile or lavender to help calm your mind and open your heart. Enter your sacred space, or find a quiet place to sit or lie down. Steady your breathing and close your eyes, if you feel comfortable. As you breathe, imagine yourself near a beach: listen to the waves flow in and out; feel the sand beneath your feet, the coolness of the water, and the brush of the breeze; smell the salt in the air. Feel the rhythm of Nature. Surrender to this calming feeling. Take time to relax and restore as you prepare for the next Moon cycle.

What excites you about a new beginning?

MOON BATHING RITUAL

Moon bathing is a simple, yet relaxing, soul-cleansing, mind-clearing ritual that can be particularly satisfying during the Waning Crescent, when the waning Moon helps us cleanse negativity from our world.

- ❯ Prepare your spot—any place you feel safe, connected to Nature, and can touch the Moon's light.

- ❯ Alternately, fill a tub with warm water. Add any salts, essential oils, flowers, or herbs you like. Place some water-friendly crystals around, or in, the bath, such as rose quartz (unconditional love, compassion, peace) or clear quartz (power) to tap into their individual energies.

- ❯ Create an altar or offering nearby, using your favorite items or special objects that relate to your intentions and that you'd like to cleanse with the Moon's energy.

- ❯ Comfortably stand or sit under the Moon's light, close your eyes, and feel your hands (if sitting) or feet firmly planted to the ground (if standing). Or, step into the tub, immerse yourself, close your eyes, and feel the water's gentle warmth and softness cradling you.

- ❯ Invite one of the crone goddesses to sit with you, so their wisdom may be absorbed along with the Moon's.

- ❯ Breathe. Deeply in. Slowly out. Again. Focus your thoughts on filling your body with the Moon's light and energy on every breath in. With every breath out, feel the energy of your breath and assess the results of your actions this past lunar cycle.

- ❯ Stay as long as you are comfortable and gently retune to the world around you when finished. Spend a moment in thanks for the Moon's guiding wisdom.

What new insights did your Moon bath reveal?

MOON MAGIC REFLECTIONS

How has working with the Moon's magical energies inspired you?

As this lunar cycle ends, what have you learned during your Moon magic journey?

How will you use what you've learned when creating new intentions for the cycle about to begin?

Date: _____   Moon Phase: _____

_____

_____

_____

_____

_____

_____

_____

_____

_____

_____

_____

_____

_____

_____

_____

_____

Inspiring | Educating | Creating | Entertaining

Brimming with creative inspiration, how-to projects, and useful information to enrich your everyday life, Quarto Knows is a favorite destination for those pursuing their interests and passions. Visit our site and dig deeper with our books into your area of interest: Quarto Creates, Quarto Cooks, Quarto Homes, Quarto Lives, Quarto Drives, Quarto Explores, Quarto Gifts, or Quarto Kids.

10 9 8 7 6 5 4 3 2

ISBN: 978-1-63106-782-2

Publisher: Rage Kindelsperger
Creative Director: Laura Drew
Managing Editor: Cara Donaldson
Editor: Keyla Pizarro-Hernández
Editorial Assistant: Alma Gomez Martinez
Cover and Interior Design: Laura Klynstra
Text: Mary J. Cassells

Printed in China